Each of the translated poems in Luísa Coelho's *Kunuar* pulses with empathy, refusing to overlook the sensory, often painful, details that animate Angola's complicated past and present. These poems, masterfully translated from the Portuguese, bridge the gap between imagination and witness; indeed, as Coelho maintains, "We are inseparable from our fiction—our traces." The translations are a treasure to any reader seeking to absorb a poetic voice resonant with both memory and incisive critique. **Elizabeth Berlinger, Managing Editor (2001-2005),** *Two Lines: World Writing in Translation* **(ekphrastic poetry)**

Some advance comments about Luísa Coelho's **Kunuar**:

How fortunate we are to have the poems of Luísa Coelho available in English through the translations of Maria do Carmo de Vasconcelos and edited by Philip Eggers. The Portuguese-speaking world is still largely an enigma to English speakers; in their dialogue with Luanda past and present, Coelho's poems plumb the language and structures that mask the complex social relations among the city's inhabitants. In an early poem, Coelho challenges a tourist with visions of a country that refuses to submit to the tidy descriptions of guidebooks. This collection, too, challenges the literary traveler to go beyond "the consumable." It is a collection that mirrors its subject's jarring juxtaposition of beauty and despair. **Eric Becker, Editor,** *Words Without Borders*

This first ever translation of Luísa Coelho's collection offers English readers a gifted poet's personal impressions of colonial and post-colonial life in Angola. Careful yet creative renderings from the Portuguese capture much lyric tension in lines that often depict rather painful subject matter. Both for its corrective of the western gaze as well as its well-crafted poetry, this book makes for necessary and enjoyable reading. **Roger Sedarat, MFA Program in Creative Writing and Literary Translation, Queens College**

Maria do Carmo de Vasconcelos's translation of Luísa Coelho's *Kunuar* makes available for the first time in English this important work by the Portuguese poet, whose 52 short poems display a fierce and penetrating sensibility in their nuanced attention to the social, political, and economic contradictions of life in Angola. Coelho's work takes its responsibilities as a poetry of witness seriously and focuses a keen eye on a world too few English-language readers have had the opportunity to experience. In these graceful and fluid translations, native Portuguese speaker de Vasconcelos accomplishes that rare feat to which all translators strive: to make from work which has moved her, poems in another language that carry enough of the sound and imagistic dynamism of the originals to exist as poems in a new language. I read *Kunar* in its English version as a compelling collection of poems that open for me a way into a world to which I would not have had access without Coelho's incisive vision and de Vasconcelos's taut and natural renderings of them. **Jim Tolan, poet, *Red Walls* and *Mass of the Forgotten***

The achingly beautiful poems in *Kunuar: Poetic Impressions of Angola* by Luísa Coelho are here translated into English by the keenly attuned Maria do Carmo de Vasconcelos. This important volume of Lusophone lyric poetry juxtaposes images of lush beauty with scenes of unbearable poverty and loss to create a testament both to the suffering and to the dignity of the people of Angola. The legacy of a cruel colonial past and a desolate post-colonial present is made vivid by Coelho's renderings, "impressions," and stark images. In "Ballet" a graceful hand gesture in the performance of hair braiding begins a dance which ends with a brutal balancing act of labor, yet in this labor we see resiliency and poise. One can imagine that the delicacy of language and the starkness of image are in themselves the result of a skilled dance between translator, de Vasconcelos, and poet, Coelho. *Kunuar* stands as a necessary contribution to the body of contemporary witness literature, and English speakers are fortunate that de Vasconcelos has chosen to render it. **Marguerite María Rivas, author of *Tell No One: Poems of Witness***

Kunuar is that rare object, a book of lyrical political poetry. It deals straight on with the colonial ruin of Angola from the point of view of an angry lover: *"Do I care about your rich natural resources/if hunger and misery are natural to you?"* The poet does not fear the unlovely. She addresses explorer David Livingstone in the midst of an attack of dysentery, and faults the victim too, the local traffic cop who "doesn't even sense that the white gloves/which conceal the black of his hands/are an ancient sign of oppression." And the poet is well aware of her own powerlessness in this realist yet melodic verse: "What remains of a stolen childhood but a/stray bullet and an amputated leg?... What remains is this sad and tired blah-blah." To be read alongside Paul Theroux's record of his recent travel there, *The Last Train to Zona Verde*. Read and weep. **Lisa Katz, editor of the Israeli domain of Poetry International Rotterdam**

Kunuar

Poetic Impressions of Angola
By
Luísa Coelho

Translated by Maria do Carmo de Vasconcelos

Editorial Advisor: Philip Eggers

Pleasure Boat Studio: A Literary Press
New York

Kunuar
By Luísa Coelho
Copyright 2015 by Luísa Coelho

All rights reserved. This book may not be reproduced, in whole or part, in any form, except by reviewers or scholars without the written permission of the publisher.
ISBN 978-0-912887-39-5
Library of Congress Control Number: 2015954887

Design and Cover by Isabel Pavão

Pleasure Boat Studio books are available through your favorite bookstore and the following:

SPD (Small Press Distribution)
Partners/West
Baker & Taylor
Ingram Book Company
Brodart
Amazon.com and bn.com

and through
PLEASURE BOAT STUDIO: A LITERARY PRESS

Contact Jack Estes, Publisher
201 West 89th Street
New York, NY 10024

pleasboat@aol.com
www.pleasureboatstudio.com

Dedication

In Memory of
Gloria Lustig

Acknowledgements

We would like to thank all our colleagues, friends, and family for their encouragement of this project.

In addition, we are grateful to former Senior Vice President Sadie Bragg and the Office of Academic Affairs at the Borough of Manhattan Community College of the City University of New York for granting released time through the Faculty Publications Program for the spring semester 2013.

Table of Contents

Introduction	XIII
Announcement	1
Letter to the Tourist	2
Ballet	4
The Fruit	5
So Much Weight on the Head	6
A Port for Discomfort	7
Mist	8
White Gloves	9
Pages from the Diary of David Livingstone, *Loanda, 14th of June, 1854*	10
Pages from the Diary of David Livingstone, *Loanda, 15th of June, 1854 (Corpus Christi)*	11
Chicken d'Angola	12
Diogo Cão and the Fortress of S. Miguel	13
Entire Afternoons	15
Natural Resources	16
Song of the Remains	17
Stray Bullet	18

The Frightened Giraffe	19
Generator	20
Litany of the Car	21
Marine Birds	22
Map of the World	23
A Screw	24
Axiluanda	25
Indifference	26
Bicycle	27
The Mask of the Dancer Tchokwe	28
The Color of the Days	29
Diary of the Loneliness of Pombeiro Pedro João Baptista	30
Window with a View of the Garbage	32
Rich Mistress of Luanda	33
Rain	34
Herbarium	35
Coin of Exchange	36
The Tail of the Dragon	37
Watch Bird	38

Potholes on the Roads	39
The Teller of Tales	40
Self Portrait of Picasso—1907	41
Beauty Salon	42
The Ring of the Serpent	43
Lemon Peel	44
Bundles of Wood	45
The Roach of the Bush	46
Musseque	47
Diary of Utilization	48
Ice Cream	49
Braided Buns	50
Friedrich Welwitsch	51
Fish Eyes	52
Philosophical Excursions	53
Flying Fish	54
Kunuar	55

Introduction

Kunuar, a book of fifty-two poems, translated from Portuguese into English, is Luísa Coelho's painful but playful re-discovery of Luanda, capital of Angola, her native country. This book was published in Brazil in 2008 and in Portugal in 2009. Coelho's empathic gaze upon the new reality of her country (independent since 1975) embodies colonial history and current personal, social and political impressions. This dialogue between past and present allows readers to feel and understand tragic elements of Angola's rich history and empathize with its destitute inhabitants' daily struggles for survival. *Kunuar* is the result of an extended dialogue between the translator and the author about the potential importance of a poetic testimony of the social situation in Luanda by an Angolan native of European descent who left the country under the oppressive Portuguese colonial order many years ago and returned to it as an independent country.

Listening to the tragicomic voices of the poems, framed by the author's feminist and post-colonial sensibilities, readers will encounter moving stories of urban ruins and ordinary people. This is reflected in the iconic image of *Kunuar*, the title of the volume as well as of the concluding poem, which refers to the small places on the street where vendors sell secondhand clothes in Luanda. These clothes are sent primarily as donations from European countries and arrive in big piles that are then spread on the ground by the shopkeepers who profit from the small purchases made by their impoverished customers. The image of a poor mother wishfully touching items of clothing on the ground as small objects of desire is presented in the poem "Kunuar". The mother, dressed in a *pano*, a colorful cotton *batik*, a traditional garment, is distraught because she cannot afford even castoff clothes, but her fury melts when the urine of her baby runs down her back and warms her. This powerful image points to many others in the collection, in which the recurrent theme of love of mother and child is one of the few sources of hope in the midst of misery and grinding poverty in a country that is the second producer of diamonds and petroleum in sub-Saharan Africa.

Like that moving and beautiful image, Coelho's poetic output exhibits other vibrant images which offer in a very subtle way an enchanting testimony about the current oppressive conditions of Luanda after four centuries of Portuguese colonial order and Angola's intense civil war from 1975 to 2002. As the Brazilian professor and literary critic Maria Nazareth Fonseca states, in her introduction to the Brazilian edition of *Kunuar*, "The memory activates the selection of the contours of the city, always described by a gaze able to restore the traces of the perverse history of colonization and the deep scars left by the interminable succession of calamities that have fallen upon the city" (11). The imagery of the ruins of the city reflects its major chronological events presented in the poems, which move in alternating rhythm between past and present: from the commerce of slaves during Portuguese colonialism, which produced class distinctions based on race and its gradations of pigmentation, to the Angolan civil war and its aftermath of thousands of Angolans, especially children, with missing limbs resulting from land mines, to the intrusion of exploitative post-colonial powers, including the Soviet Union, and finally to the depredations of global capitalism with the advent of international corporations.

Again, the indictment of those injustices in Coelho's poems is the result of her love for her African land as well as her familiarity with its colonial and post-colonial experiences. In the center of her poetic output is the symbol of the big, overpopulated and impoverished capital in a country rich in natural resources. Her descriptions are variations of similar scenes that are scrutinized and deconstructed by a gaze that falls on the indigent general population in contrast to the very wealthy few. This picture of inequality mirrors the desolate visions of the present which flash back to other scenarios recaptured by memory pervading the verse lines that reproduce "words never heard before." In this sense, Coelho gives voice to a colonial time that has not been a prevalent theme in Portuguese poetics. The gaze that conjures up memory allows for a vivid dialogue between today and yesterday in a very competent way that allows both poet and reader to share and ultimately research the remains of Luanda's history for both to understand and transmit their newfound knowledge.

A few examples can illustrate this process. The first poem of the collection, "Anúncio" ("Announcement"), brings us back to the time of the commerce of slaves. This poem, to a certain extent, establishes a conversation with the poem "Carta ao Turista" ("Letter to the Tourist"); the two poems allude to different times and are written in dissimilar poetic genres—declaration and epistolary modes, respectively. "Anúncio" is an invitation to the reader to visit, imaginatively and in an empathic manner, terrible oppressive eras with tragic realities hidden from the large African population, such as the localized selling of slaves and the dismantling of villages, ethnic groups, and families. Similarly, the verse lines in "Carta ao Turista" offer a catalogue of pleasures for the tourist, but the real, painful history of the country is as hidden from today's tourists, who are in search of souvenirs and the beauty of the beaches, as were the secrets of colonial times from Portuguese representatives of the colonial order.

The dialectic between colonial suffering and the rigors of post-colonial survival is sensitively depicted in lovely, impressionistic and hopeful scenes of individuals who are dreaming of a future in the midst of insuperable obstacles. For instance, a poor security guard, who sleeps standing up supposedly protecting a room in a hotel, ironically and naively reveals his dreams of possessing African animals and just one screw to be able to close the door to his house so he can finally enjoy real sleep. The hardships in this poem, and throughout the collection, are depicted through metonymy and personification, which are also inseparable from the poverty, misery, and filth of present day Luanda. For example, "cracked feet stamped through filth" and "flies that suck his feet"—these metonyms allude to the broken existence of an entire population with almost no future; however, small glimpses of a woman braiding her hair, singing lullabies to her children, or selling vegetables in the open air market point to hope in the midst of extremely difficult political and socio-economic realities. Despite the country's significant economic development since political stability was achieved in 2002, especially due to the fast rising earnings of the oil sector, the country faces serious social and economic problems. These and other tragic predicaments in the history of Angola caused by the slave trade, four centuries of Portuguese colonial order, and a quarter century of civil war are the fabric of Coelho's *Kunuar* which deserves to be shared by an English-speaking audience. Witnessing this oppressed human landscape will result in a kind of cathartic experience for the readers.

The cultural gap caused by the omission of Portuguese writing from English-speaking discourse is eloquently reflected in the following quotation: "What the English don't know is the Africa which speaks and writes in Portuguese and French," said José Eduardo Agualusa, a best-selling 55-year-old Angolan author and winner of the Portuguese Grand Prize for Literature as well as the Independent Foreign Fiction Prize in the United Kingdom in 2007 for his novel, *The Book of Chameleons*. As he commented in an interview, "It's a prize for translation in a country where, like in the U.S., people don't read much translation."(http://wordswithoutborders.org/article/an-interview-with-jos-eduardo-agualusa/#ixzz1GdFfvphc).

Hence, the translation of Coelho's *Kunuar*, whose initial concept for the book of Portuguese poems originated in conversations between the translator and the author, will respond to this urgent need for Lusophone literature in English translation. National and international audiences will have access to the culture and socio-politics of an African country that has been lagging behind in relation to the Anglophone or even Francophone parts of Africa. As Agualusa's remarks illuminate, the reason is to be found in its cultural isolation, partially due to the language barrier. "Scholars and institutions communicating in Portuguese have virtually been unknown in the mainstream, [a practice which has been] internationally accepted, and English [has] dominated [the] evolution of concepts and practices in population and development in Africa" (*Rural Women, Population and Development in Lusophone Africa; Annotated Bibliography 4*).

Kunuar might lift the veil on the place where colonial and postcolonial history meets poetics, divulging these Portuguese gems.

– Maria do Carmo de Vasconcelos

Kunuar

Announcement

I notify whomever it may concern:
there exists on deposit
in the public jail of Luanda a runaway female slave
named Ngunja with her little brood
captured in Cambambe who claims to belong
to a man from Ambaca
named Quinjige.

The owner is requested to come forward and identify the mark
that is tattooed on her hip
and profit from the arrival in port of a caravel
bringing a good Christian who wishes nothing more
than to buy what he has there.

Letter to the Tourist

You ask that I speak to you about this land,
but nothing would get us anywhere
if I spoke to you of the curve of the bay, of the road stretching around it,
of the tall palm trees that wave to it, of the sand island which confronts it,
of the lighthouse that guides the boats,
of the small feminine hills which give it form.

From the top of the veranda of your hotel room,
in lands never visited by me,
you already saw these images projected
innumerable times onto a fabricated scenario.
But if I would dare
I would be able then to tell you
that when the afternoon declines into evening,
when the rapid sun dives into the red of the sea,
for moments the forms of silvery mermaids can be seen
or that at the dawn,
when the sun's rays inundate the orange of the small hills,
for moments the ephemeral tracks can be seen
of winged women.
I would, however, be fabulating
and, dear tourist,
only the programmed reality interests you.

To speak to you of the cool rooms of the hotels, with tables laden with
        gourmet specialties, of the
famous stretches of white sand and of the shady beaches with waters
tepid and blue,
this, yes, would comfort you.

To tell you that you can be stuffed with the fake arts and crafts of wood,
of Dutch-dyed cloths, Chinese watches,
Lebanese carpets and even,
with some luck, of one
squatted
tired
forgotten
native thinker.
It would be an illusion, however, to tell you
that all that this land has is consumable
because its great richness, that which charms,
doesn't present itself to you as an available article.

Ballet

Early in the morning, when she wakes up, always this first gesture:
the ballet of the hand on the design of the braids of the hair
only afterward to send flying over the street the odor that escapes from the
        bucket of urine
to cover the body with a cloth, that blue one with orange and white flowers,
to place with great tenderness her sleeping son on her back
to balance cans of soda in a cardboard box on her head.
To hit the road and carry on life as if the world were just and a hairdo
were enough to nourish the soul.

The Fruit

It was on that day like so many others with clouds covering the sun
        and ash-colored light
that for the first time I saw you:

The reticent look of someone who experiences misery
with the clenched fists of someone who conceals,
the cracked feet of someone who stamps the filth,
the tightly closed lips of someone who no longer wants to talk.

And the colors of that scented fruit
in the sisal basket
are always and always
trying to divert
my gaze.

So Much Weight on the Head

How can you
walk barefoot in water from the sewers
scavenge leftovers of food amidst the garbage
give your withered breast to the son who is going to die
open your legs to the violence of a drunkard
drink the water that the land didn't want
survive the fever bitten on the skin
eat fish covered with flies
dance your sorrows on the beach sand
under the full moon
clean the sleep crust from the eyes of children with your own spit
wash clothes without clean water
make yourself beautiful without the magic of a mirror
pick lice from the hair of others
give strength to the eldest in their walking
sleep on the floor with roaches and mice
breed a child every year
bury the legs of children that jump on the mines
satiate the hunger of the youngest on your breasts
carry so much weight on your head
start to smile when I ask you the price of the mangoes

open my eyes, woman, and explain to me how you can
because there are days when I'm the one who cannot bear it.

A Port for Discomfort

I remember having walked by here
sometimes there are images that come to me
in flocks of flamingoes in the mangrove
in phosphorescent seaweed among the waves
in small conch shells that wave to me in a spiral
in children who steal green mangoes
in dogs that stretch themselves leisurely
in twilights that suddenly go out
in fireflies that illuminate the yard.

Sometimes there are memories that come to me
in words never heard before
in gestures that are learned in a moment
in messages whispered by the winds
in ships that arrive late at the port
in odors of acacias that turn orange
in echoes of other voices repeated
in tongues which I have never heard.

I remember having walked by here
at a time that I still do not remember.

Mist

And suddenly it is as if you were still there:

I watch the salt of the sea emerging in mist from your mouth
and the pink of the flamingo flying in your gaze.

White Gloves

Dandy
the traffic cop doesn't even sense that the white gloves
which conceal the black of his hands
are an ancient sign of oppression.

Pages from the Diary of David Livingstone
Loanda 14th of June 1854

Under the spreading tree of this white house
inhabited by Gabriel Edmond,
in the elevated city of Loanda
with my butt propped over a basin with the steam from boiling water
I frighten away the diarrhea and make the intermittent African fever
      evaporate,
they are pills of opium and of tamed dragon
with quinine,
a mix of laudanum,
tincture of rubber and magnesium
and on the tongue the sour taste of the fedigueira plant.

In my perspiring memory
humid biblical images pass by
projected by the magic lantern on the wall of the hut,
the obsession of the meeting with the source of the Nile,
the first crocodile eggs,
rocky gorges that drop into
lakes of sparkling waters
the astonished eyes of Mary
drowned in alcohol.

At the end, in the flushed reflection of the heat of the bay,
I observe the shadow of a fleet that the twilight distances.
The mad screams that I hear
are not mine, no,
they are born from the waters and the school of fish running away,
they are from the slaves that the cargo hold swallowed.

Pages from the Diary of David Livingstone

Loanda 15th of June 1854 (Corpus Christi)

Kneel get up go down
sit incline cross yourself
whisper and sing.
The ritual that the Makololo,
my fellow travelers,
observed curiously at the mass of Corpus Christi
in the church of St. Peter in the high city of Loanda.
What did you most find strange?
That the bishop,
after whetting their appetite with promises
made in mysterious Latin words
and solemn gestures,
at the precise moment when the revelation would be announced to them,
would turn his back on them.

Chicken d'Angola

Early in the morning, with the door of the coop opened,
pardon, of the classroom,
the first that emerges is the chicken
followed by the chicks
they are seven
all night they slept cradled
by the waves of the verses of medieval poetry
that we left floating in the room
since the last class of the day before.

Already outside, in the sun, while pecking the dust,
cackling in a choir love songs medieval,
excuse me, I mean, animal.

Diogo Cão and the Fortress of S. Miquel*

At the door of the fort I heard voices, entered,
ran into you unburdening yourself,
you spoke of those nights in which the moon torments you
and makes you digress.
Faced with the warlike torpor of the cuban planes
and the russian snoring of the cars without combat
the moon makes your tired eyelids flutter and murmurs,
slowly,
echoing:
"Diogo, explorer of the old sea, unfurl the sails, let's navigate."
You look with your gaze at impassive Gama who dozes at the end,
you evoke a precious assistance—
you ask him to prevent you from leaving.

In your feet you still feel the fine sand and much desire to return
but you know nonetheless, Diogo my friend, that the king is not ready
        to forgive.
To confuse an uninhabited and foggy cape with the end of the continent
is an unforgivable error in this kingdom.
The ambassador confessed to the pope
that the world was about to change,
the maritime way to India was at hand.
Many favors were granted to you,
patterns were engraved on your coat of arms,
promises of guaranteed honors,
how can you retreat now?

A tiger approaches cautiously and you already feel him sniffing,
eye to eye the courages are measured
affinities are met.
On the stretch of sand you advance mounted on the back of that beast,
you defend your truth.

Awakened by the noise of your memories
the cuban airplane questions itself, perplexed:
"But after all who are you, hero of stone, that dares to awaken me like this?"
"I was a planter of stone markers without end
who having dared to shorten the dimensions of the world,
venturing into the forest I became entangled
and from there I never returned.
I rest now imprisoned
in the fortress inscribed in these lands bathed by the sea
that I once opened."
"What do you bring then rolled up in your hand?"
inquires the incredulous flying machine.
"It is only the envied itinerary of the innovating voyage,
the proof that the continent grew up while I was away."
And it was at this moment that the cuban plane took advantage of the open
       window
and flew away.

---

*Diogo Cão and the fortress—The sculptures of historical figures that the Portuguese left in Luanda were taken off the streets and placed inside the fortress of the city.

Entire Afternoons

You never left my memory,
in entire afternoons of pleasurable chat
and painful charges.
I was inventing you the way I needed you.
And now that I have you,
here I am
giving an account to the world
of your nonexistence.

What to make of a time that neither left any trace nor occupied any space?

Natural Resources

Do I care about your rich natural resources
if hunger and misery are natural to you?
Do I care about the petroleum, the diamonds, the iron, the magnesium, the
    copper,
the phosphates, the granite, the marble, the rare minerals, the precious
    woods,
the energy of the rivers,
if that young man trembling with fever in the heat of the day
knocks on the glass of my car window
and tirelessly extends to me his empty hands.

Song of the Remains

What remains of a stolen childhood but a
stray bullet and an amputated leg?

What remains of a stolen bullet but an
amputated childhood and a missing leg?

What remains of a stolen leg but a
lost childhood and an amputated bullet?

What remains is this sad and tired blah-blah.

Stray Bullet

I used to see him looking fixedly
in the garbage scattered on the ground
for the stray bullet which had stolen his vision.
All that he expected from life
was one day to be able to see it.

The Frightened Giraffe

The fault is all yours
for a long time I haven't stopped thinking of you

whenever a bird falls
without a vacancy on the twig
a fire is reflected
in the eyes of the gazelle
a felled tree
assaults the landscape
a destroyed bridge
prevents passage
a house in ruins
forgets its name
a frightened giraffe
stops to peek
a violated woman
hides herself humiliated
a foot that is already gone
searches for a boot
a child lying on the bed
does not even extend her arms to me
a baobab tree
divides in half to me
an entire city
drowns in urine

a group that passes by
threatens

for a long time I haven't stopped thinking of you,
the fault is all yours.

Generator

Only later did I know that he committed suicide.
It was impossible for him to live alone
in the silence caused
by the inexplicable muteness of his electric generator.

Litany of the Car

The young people of the street wash the cars with stolen water.

The owners of the cars pay the young people of the street who wash the
> cars with
stolen water.

The owners of the houses that are on the streets where the
> owners of the cars pay
the young people of the street who wash the cars with stolen water,
rent the hoses.

The sons of the owners of the houses that are on the streets where the
> owners of the cars
pay the young people of the street who wash the cars with stolen water and
> who
rent the hoses
watch the number of cars that each young person of the street washes.

The sellers of sodas, who are on the streets where the owners of
the cars pay the young people of the street who wash the cars with stolen
> water,
who rent the hoses and watch the number of cars that each young person of
the street washes, sell drinks to the sons of the owners of the houses.

But no one can steal from the young people of the street the illusion that
> they are
the owners of the cars that they wash with stolen water.

Marine Birds

And to our names
others were added
and others came
and all listened.
It was on the shore
on the point of Restinga:
"I will never come back here"—I swore to the marine birds,
pensive lighthouse keepers (the only ones that recognized me),
speaking for my whole generation.

But the only thing that calms me down is
the past echo of that salty gaze.

Map of the World

Nova Lisboa is Huambo
Sá da Bandeira, Lubango
Novo Redondo is the Sumbe
Salazar, Ndlatando
Luso became Luena
Moçâmedes is the Namibe
Teixeira de Sousa, Luau
Silva Porto is the Kuito

And the child of long ago
is I
a foreigner in that which is also mine.

A Screw

At the door of my hotel room in Luanda,
a security guard sleeps standing up.
With open unmoving eyes,
all night he protects the path walked in his dreams.
I try not to wake him.
Early in the morning, he thanks me serenely for the good day I wish him:
—Thank you, godmother.
With the expressive, rosy palms of his immense hands
drawn with dark rivers
he tells me the story of the man who believes in the future:
—I want to have an enormous alligator, two turtle eggs, a mug of
purée of corn and a screw.
—A screw?
—To close the door of my house and be able to sleep.

Axiluanda*

Of all the children she bred, Maria loved the first the most.
Who, inside a canoe, wrapped in a piece of cloth,
had been given as an offering to the sea and had given back fish
        in abundance.
Every night the eyes delved in that immensity
wet and dark without end and felt
that to be a mother was to have the power
to dominate the sea without even knowing how to swim.

---

*Axiluanda—Sons of Luanda, the name given to the first inhabitants of the Island of Luanda, fishermen.

Indifference

Lying on the waves of the pattern of stones on the street at the shore of the
        bay, numbed,
not even swatting the flies which suck his feet.
He ignores them.
His dream is to be minister, to have a jeep and eat meat every day.
The flies—screw them. They don't have an important position, they don't
        have a car,
and they don't eat meat.
Only suck blood.

Bicycle

This night Bento has dreamt that he would be able to make his nightmare come true.
He has decided, then, to fill his bicycle tire with air and head out to conquer it.
It was his only way to liberate himself from it.

The Mask of the Dancer Tchokwe

While alive we cannot escape from the masks and the names.
We are inseparable from our fiction—our traces.
We are condemned to invent a mask to discover later
that the mask is our true face.
                                    Octávio Paz

The heavy mask of wood of the dancer tchokwe
is the face that she doesn't have
it has enormous eyes with little slits by which she doesn't see
it has the nose of the bird, hooked, by which she doesn't smell
it has the mouth of the thick closed lips by which she doesn't speak
it has the long thick hair of sisal through which she can't breathe.
She dances, she spins, wrapped in a cloud of dust and letting loose
        blasphemies stamping
furiously with her feet on the ground of red soil, shaking her skirts
of straw to the sound of the beating of the tambours, exhibiting the black of
        her thighs in
intervals of drumbeats.
The mask of wood of the dancer tchokwe
is her greatest force of expression.

The Color of the Days

The day always awakes in ashen,
the light itself is humid and warm, the sun hidden by the clouds dares,
knows that we don't yet have strength to protest.

The day always ends in a light blue sky
scratched over in red orange rose,
in a sun of profound transparency
tranquil harmony of one who doesn't even need to dare,
because it always leaves us
an immense willingness
to begin again.

Diary of the Loneliness of Pombeiro*
Pedro João Baptista

São Paulo da Assunção de Luanda, 25th of July 1806

In the name of God Amen

•

Defeat that I, João Pedro Baptista, make of my trip
from Muropue for the King Cazembe of Caquinhata for the opening of the way
to the eastern coast of Africa.

•

Tuesday the fifth of July we got up at the first cock's crow with light
rain we passed by four narrow rivulets of running water
we arrived at a place where a black was saying Ave Marias we always went
    with the sun on
our back we didn't have any disturbance and we met
no one.

•

Wednesday the sixth of July we got up at three in the morning and we went
    always walking
close to the rivulet three fathoms wide and a dead doe was left for us
and manioc and we continued with the sun the same way and saw
nothing.

•

Thursday the seventh of July we sailed at six in the morning and exchanged two small
mirrors and a few dyed cotton fabrics for extra supplies
we stopped for the night outdoors in the rainy season and
met no one.

•

Friday the eighth of July we got up at dawn passed by a river and en-
countered ten blacks who had gone to buy salt and walked
with the sun on our left side and we saw nothing at all.

"But after all who were you searching for, Pedro João,
that amidst so many encounters you were able to meet
no one?"

---

*Pombeiro—a merchant slave. João Pedro Baptista was a slave of Francisco Honorato da Costa, director of the market of Cassengue—a fortified post east of Luanda where the commerce with the interior of Angola was centralized.

Window with a View of the Garbage

I have a window with a view of the garbage
of butterflies with yellow wings
in which peep eyes of indigo;

circling over the greasy and dark waters
that trickle through the open sewer into the veins of the city
fluttering by the cracked walls, by the broken windows,
by the blood, by the excrement,
they never dirty the immaculate colors
with which they dress themselves.

I have a window that looks onto the hope which dances in the eyes drawn
on the wings of the butterflies.

Rich Mistress of Luanda*

Now that through the windows of your beautiful nineteenth-century
    mansion no longer
escape
the sound of the steps of the rhythmical quadrille, the very obscene
    contortions
of massemba, the deaf protests of the slaves, the shouted orders in
quimbundo, the moanings of pleasure of the caresses without loving
    words, the
clouds of white talcum liberated from the wigs, the odors of the heaps
of chicken with peanuts, the discussion of the dark business of slave ships,
the voices of the readings of the announcements of the fugitive and
    recaptured slaves, the
betrayals and denunciations of the colonial power, the hoarse howls of the
    corporal
punishments,
you, Ana Joaquina, rich mistress of Luanda, are more present than ever.

The emptiness of your palace makes even more visible what is impossible
to hide.

---

* D. Ana Joaquina—a lady of the creole society of Luanda in the 19th century, mestiza, rich and educated, in whose mansion the bourgeoisie of that era would meet.

Rain

When the rain stops, the multicolored wings of millions of
butterflies flutter, the silk spiders, suspended in invisible trapezes,
swing from branch to branch,
the snore of the cicadas recommences to stun the air
the wasps shake their wet wings
and peek from the nests of clay.

But it is at six o'clock in the afternoon that the sun disappears,
the muddy land dives into the shade,
the insects retire
and all becomes silent.

Throughout the night, millions of dry eyes continue to count,
in the dark,
the dead and the disappeared that the violence of the waters
evaporated.

Herbarium

The mist that had darkened the horizon then, in large
and stretched rags allowing one to perceive through the spaces in the
        contours of
the faraway lands, a vegetal painting

palm-of-christ, aloe,
hemp, rubber, coffee,
peanuts, peppers, cotton,
rice, papaya, dragon's-blood,
corn, sorghum, palm tree,
elemi balsam, poppy,
massango, castor oil, cashew,
sucupira, anil, guava,
anona, cinnamon, mafumeira tree,
manioc, avocado, camellia,
chili, dendém.

Coin of Exchange

And they picked up calabashes full to the brim with salt,
bracelets of gold-colored metal, fabrics the pasty color of chalk,
hoops of copper to entangle the ankles,
buttons made of bone for shirts, pearls—black or white,
conches of moist skin like frogs or shells—snails or olives.

And most of all they held, very carefully, the cowrie shells
white or light yellow the size of an almond
brought as ballast in the ships that docked from the Indies
and they smoothed with the palm of their hand their convex dorsal valve
and felt with the fingertips
the roughness of the edge of the torn slit
and they tasted their odor
and perforated them
and strung them up
in necklaces
and the funantes* departed
mounted on the backs of bulls into the bush
certain that their coin of exchange was fragilely precious

---

*Funantes—wandering vendors who in Angola transported the most varied goods and who roamed from settlement to settlement doing their business.

The Tail of the Dragon

My beloved, let us bury the painful memories and let
the ruins of the houses of cement, the blood that drips down the walls of
adobe, the gutted banks of the plazas, the dry fountains of the gardens, the
        streets
potholed, the dusty paths and mined forests of acacias fill
themselves
with red blossoms of bougainvillea
of serpents of one thousand heads
of laughs that echo at the bottom of the rivers
so that tomorrow we can separate ourselves again in peace.

For we alone know that the rainbow is only the tail of the dragon.

Watch Bird

It is ultra marine the love of the sea serpent
for the worm of the guava.
And it is for that that the serpent,
which lives right there in the belly of the stones that adorn the bay,
quite early in the morning,
when the worm still sleeps, hidden on the moist bark of the ripe guava,
slithers sinuously through the beach sands
crosses the dunes, glides up to the wooden veranda of the house of Bina
starts slowly and silently to waltz by the trunk of the guava,
assured that her love doesn't betray her.
And if it were not for the noisy tweeting of the watch bird,
who knows how many seconds the worm of the guava would have
to feel in its skin the certainty of her serpentine love.

Potholes on the Roads

On all the roads
waves of indefatigable Chinese
cover
uncover
recover
the holes
rice-harvesting hats
long sleeves
high collars à la Mao
covered bodies without shape
the pallor of faces red from the soil
are not a mirage
are the discord of the world in transit.
New missionaries of oil.

The Teller of Tales

It was on a night of stars,
once upon a time in the sea,
there was that honey-colored light
grooved by the sweating of the waves
and the very silence of one who overhears words
fantasizing castles on the sea.
And it was in the dialogue cradled by the rhythm,
that the teller of tales would dance, the listener would dance,
that the boat overturned
and the story shipwrecked.

It is comfortable not having a past
to be able to invent it.
It was from that shipwreck on that I started to lie to you
and to tell that my country
has the smell of the sea water.

Self Portrait of Picasso – 1907

At dawn Picasso sees himself, one last time,
in the enigma of the African mask.

The revelation happens,
He recognizes himself:
a high forehead, enormous bronzed eyes with a fixed gaze,
fine, dark eyebrows,
a long nose, large at the base,
a mouth with thick lips,
prominent ears,
brown wooden skin,
in an image which expels evils, protects the initiated, keeps the
order and the harmony

He understands calmly that the mask dilutes the anguish,
causes perplexity,
prevents the worst failure:
not to live.

Beauty Salon

It is on that very street, in the shade of the baobab,
that Juca shaves the hair
of his cousins
a limping plastic chair
scissors with missing teeth
a chunk of cut mirror
but the most loyal clients
are the goats
they surveil all around
they don't leave any leftovers from the flying kinky clumps
that land on the dusty ground.

The Ring of the Serpent

He sat on the curb
and from the plastic bag
conjured up
a ring of serpent's skin
an ostrich egg
a head support
a comb.
Suspended in the dust from the ground
they already have the smell of bread.

Lemon Peel

Luanda is kind of weird.

She comes to us as if she is lost
through the slums of mud
bottled laziness
pressed in the narrow streets
occupied by vendors
scaffolded in naked plazas
trimmed by ruins.

Haughty and divine
she empties into a sea breeze,
made pure.

Luanda pierces like pocket knives
lures like honey

without dogs that fornicate
birds that sing
lamps that illuminate
faucets that pour
sewers that evacuate
dust that sits on the ground

with children that play on the garbage
pigs that peek at the streets
goats that balance on dusty knolls
distance running chickens
rumps that are hoisted without trembling.

Luanda has a lemon peel
—wrinkled smoothness.

Bundles of Wood

There are days like this
in which along the curb of the dusty road
they walk in single file
enormous heads of bundled wood
heads of plasticized water
blue
yellow
red,
bodies of women wrapped in colors
without faces
without neurasthenia without depression
without hysteria or prostration.

Days like this are every day.

The Roach of the Bush

Envious of the roach of the bush
the hunting spider spins an invisible geometrical web
perfect
and pretends that she doesn't even peek at the roach.

Musseque*

In a certain moon,
at birth,
after having erred
during the day
through the raving of the slum
already in bed
maybe I curl up with you,
in a little shell,
and whisper to you, still dizzy, in your ear:
astonishment.

It is the cleanest word that can pass through my lips.
Where do they go to get the strength to survive this way?

---

*Musseques are extremely poor neighborhoods in the periphery of Luanda.

Diary of Utilization

Milk of papaya whitens
the clothing
a stick from Cabinda stirs
the desire
chili peppers from the Congo season
the chicken
powder of rhinoceros horn removes poison
from the blood
eye of viper heals
the abscess
a wooden amulet with a human figure improves
everything
grilled liver of the billy goat marinated in strong vinegar cures
a derangement of the stomach
manure of goat well sifted alleviates
the pain in the stomach

only your existence does not fulfill
mine.

Ice Cream

Seated on the potholed sidewalk
in the stripes of shade combed by the wind
legs open and feet extended
you protect between your robust and warm thighs
the cold ice cream
which doesn't melt,
in your opinion,
only because it won't.
—No, Ma'am, it ain't no mystery, it won't melt.

Braided Buns

Your body of mud
with legs imprisoned in the torrent
whose fury flattens the hut
doesn't try to save the foam mattress
or the plastic chair
swept out to sea,
your hands hold the head of a woman sculpted in the memory of the wood:

the kinky hair tidied in braided buns is all that is left for you of Esmeralda.

Friedrich Welwitsch*

From the prestigious Viennese world of theater criticism
to the botanical garden of Coimbra,
to the sweet herbs of the gardens of Lumiar of the Duke of Palmela
to the lands of the medicinal drugs of florae angolensi
and of the samples of exotic scented wood
you arrived
with fever, scurvy, dysentery and ulcers in the legs
at the desert of Namibe,
you looked and saw:
a fabulous being of the vegetal world:
a gigantic millenarian octopus guardian of impossible stretches of sand.

Only one trace,
two enormous, long and narrow olive-green leaves
in strips
scissored by the wind,
ribbons of other Carnavals:
Tombua was her name.
The gazes melted
they became Welwitschia.
You made evident the beauty
of all ugly creatures.

---

*Friedrich Welwitsch was an Austrian botanist who discovered a plant in the desert of Namibe which was afterwards baptized with his name.

Fish Eyes

From the blue plastic wash basin
balanced on the head of the fisherwoman from the Island
the wild-eyed fish
peek at the tips of the avocados
rested on the ground
and at the nipples of the breasts
squashed in the shirts of the buyers
who discuss the price:
—"A thousand kwanza? I'll only give five hundred, sister!"
Offended,
the fish pretend to be dead and
their eyes glaze over.

Philosophical Excursions*

Cacolo, Caconda, Catumbela,
Cameia, Calandula, Camabatela,
Cubal, Cunene, Cacongo,
Cacula, Camacupa, Capelongo
Mussende, Mussulo, Muxima,
Cacuzo, Cahama, Caála
Catchiungo, Bailundo, Quibala
Montipa, Matala, Zala,
Cabinda, Cainde,
Caluquembe, Cambambe,
Camaxilo, Balombo,
Sombo, Cazombo, Sanza Pombo,
Bibala, Gabela, Maquela do Zombo,
Negage, Chiluage,
Chiange, Malanje,
Caraculo, Calulo, Andulo,
Cucumbi, Sacacama, Catabola,

with so much sonority
curled in the rotundity of my mouth,
it is with closed eyes that I draw you
on the map of my childhood.

---

*Philosophical excursions was the name given to the expeditions that took place in the 18th century to Africa and Brazil organized by a team of scientists to study the local geography, ethnography, fauna and flora.

Flying Fish

The riscador* observed attentively
the flying fish caught during the Atlantic crossing
and preserved in spirits of wine.
He drew it with the sharpened point of a pencil
covered the lines with black ink
with the point of a quill pen
applied gradations of colors
which he allowed to dry.

*"This exercise uninterrupted for two months,
if it will not produce any other effect,
gives to the most rebellious hand that art of whittling
denied to some by nature."*

---

*Riscador was the name given to the draftsmen who, during the philosophical voyages, were required to reproduce everything that it was impossible to transport or describe.

Kunuar*

Bent over the lives
that the mountains of used clothes draw
on the red soil of the market of Roque Santeiro,
Honorata leafs through secondhand stories.
And only she knows why she laughs:
it is from the love
she feels
branded on her, tooth and nail.
Her baby,
snuggled in the cloth,
inhabits her back
and the warmth of the urine running down
softens her rage against the lack of kwanzas.**

---

*Kunuar is the name given in Luanda to the places on the street where the clothing that arrives in bales is scattered on the ground and sold.
**The kwanza is the currency of Angola introduced following Angolan independence. It replaced the Portuguese escudo.

About the author

Luísa Coelho, born in Angola, has Portuguese nationality. She holds a B.A. in Germanic Philology from the Classic University of Lisbon, an M.A. in Political Philosophy from the Portuguese Catholic University, and a Ph.D. in Portuguese Studies from the University of Utrecht, Holland. She did postdoctoral work in Post-Colonial Studies in the South Atlantic (Portugal-Angola-Brazil) at the University of Bologna, Italy. She has taught in several countries, including Holland, Austria, France, Brazil, and Angola. Since 2010 she has been teaching Portuguese language, culture, and literature at the Freie Universität and Humboldt Universität in Berlin, Germany.

About the translators

Maria do Carmo Allen de Vasconcelos-Eggers and **Philip Eggers** hold Ph.Ds in English and are professors of English at the Borough of Manhattan Community College of the City University of New York. Dr. de Vasconcelos was born in Portugal, grew up in Lourenço Marques (now Maputo), Mozambique, and spent time in Luanda, London, Munich, Paris, Jakarta, Denpasar, and other cities. Along with degrees from the National Conservatory of Lisbon and from the Classic University of Lisbon, where she also completed postgraduate studies in American Culture and Literature, she received certificates in language, literature, art, and philosophy from various other European universities. In New York City, she also trained in conflict resolution, completed studies in gender, race, ethnicity, and sexuality, and earned a Ph.D. from the City University of New York Graduate Center. Previously, with Dr. Dolores Deluise, she translated the novella *Monique* by Luísa Coelho into English from the Portuguese. Dr. Eggers, a native of Indiana, received his B.A. from Columbia College and his M.A. and Ph.D. in English and Comparative Literature from Columbia University. For eighteen years he was the elected chairperson of the English Department at the Borough of Manhattan Community College. Dr. de Vasconcelos and Dr. Eggers teach a variety of writing and literature courses, including world literature, post-colonial literature, the short story, modern poetry, autobiography and many others. They have published articles, scholarly books, textbooks, and translations. Together they are proficient in a number of European languages. Their careers and destiny brought them together; they are married and enjoy working together and exploring the U.S.A., other countries and cultures.

Poetry Books from
Pleasure Boat Studio: A Literary Press
Listed by release date

Seaglass Picnic • Frances Driscoll
Domain of Silence/Domain of Absence • Louis Phillips
Headwaters • Saul Weisberg
House of Burnt Offerings • Judith Skillman
Poems from Ish River Country • Robert Sund
The Juried Heart • James Clarke
The Whiskey Epiphanies • Dick Bakken
For My Father • Amira Thoron
Return to a Place Like Seeing • John Palmer
Ascendance • Tim McNulty
Lawyer Poets and That World We Call Law • Ed. James Elkins
Alter Mundus • Lucia Gizzino • trans. from Italian by Michael Daley
The Every Day • Sarah Plimpton
A Taste • Morty Schiff
Dark Square • Peter Marcus
Notes from Disappearing Lake • Robert Sund
Taos Mountain • Paintings, poetry • Robert Sund
A Path to the Sea • Liliana Ursu, trans. from Romanian by Adam J. Sorkin and Tess Gallagher
Songs from a Yahi Bow: Poems about Ishi • Yusef Komanyakaa, Mike O'Connor, Scott Ezell
Beautiful Passing Lives • Edward Harkness
Immortality • Mike O'Connor
Painting Brooklyn • Paintings by Nina Talbot, Poetry by Esther Cohen
Ghost Farm • Pamela Stewart
Unknown Places • Peter Kantor, trans. from Hungarian by Michael Blumenthal
Moonlight in the Redemptive Forest • Michael Daley • includes a CD
Jew's Harp • Walter Hess
The Light on Our Faces • Lee Whitman-Raymond
God Is a Tree • Esther Cohen
Home & Away: Old Town Poems • Kevin Miller
Against Romance • Michael Blumenthal

Days We Would Rather Know • Michael Blumenthal
Craving Water • Mary Lou Sanelli
When the Tiger Weeps • Mike O'Connor
Concentricity • Sheila E. Murphy
The Immigrant's Table • Mary Lou Sanelli
Women in the Garden • Mary Lou Sanelli
Saying the Necessary • Edward Harkness
Nature Lovers • Charles Potts
The Politics of My Heart • William Slaughter
The Rape Poems • Frances Driscoll

The following books are from Empty Bowl Press, a Division of Pleasure Boat Studio

Glenolden Park • Richard Lloyd
Hanoi Rhapsodies • Scott Ezell
P'u Ming's Oxherding Pictures & Verses • trans. from Chinese by Red Pine
Swimming the Colorado • Denise Banker
Lessons Learned • Finn Wilcox
Petroglyph Americana • Scott Ezell
Old Tale Road • Andrew Schelling
Working the Woods, Working the Sea • Eds. Finn Wilcox, Jerry Gorsline
The Blossoms Are Ghosts at the Wedding • Tom Jay • with essays
Desire • Jody Aliesan
Dreams of the Hand • Susan Goldwitz
The Basin: Poems from a Chinese Province • Mike O'Connor
The Straits • Michael Daley
In Our Hearts and Minds: The Northwest and Central America • Ed. Michael Daley
The Rainshadow • Mike O'Connor
Untold Stories • William Slaughter

Our Chapbook Series

No. 1: *The Handful of Seeds: Three and a Half Essays* • Andrew Schelling
No. 2: *Original Sin* • Michael Daley
No. 3: *Too Small to Hold You* • Kate Reavey
No. 4: *The Light on Our Faces* – re-issued in non-chapbook (see above list)
No. 5: *Eye* • William Bridges
No. 6: *Selected New Poems of Rainer Maria Rilke* • trans. fm German by Alice Derry
No. 7: *Through High Still Air: A Season at Sourdough Mountain* • Tim McNulty
No. 8: *Sight Progress* • Zhang Er, trans. from Chinese by Rachel Levitsky
No. 9: *The Perfect Hour* • Blas Falconer
No. 10: *Fervor* • Zaedryn Meade
No. 11: *Some Ducks* • Tim McNulty
No. 12: *Late August* • Barbara Brackney
No. 13: *The Right to Live Poetically* • Emily Haines

From other publishers (in limited editions)

In Blue Mountain Dusk • Tim McNulty • Broken Moon Press
China Basin • Clemens Starck • Story Line Press
Journeyman's Wages • Clemens Starck • Story Line Press

Orders: Pleasure Boat Studio books are available by order from your bookstore, directly from our website, or through the following:
SPD (Small Press Distribution) Tel. 8008697553, Fax 5105240852
Partners/West Tel. 4252278486, Fax 4252042448
Baker & Taylor 8007751100, Fax 8007757480
Ingram Tel 6157935000, Fax 6152875429
Amazon.com or Barnesandnoble.com

Pleasure Boat Studio: A Literary Press
201 West 89th Street
New York, NY 10024
www.pleasureboatstudio.com / pleasboat@nyc.rr.com

www.ingramcontent.com/pod-product-compliance
Lightning Source LLC
Chambersburg PA
CBHW052029290426
44112CB00014B/2438